POSTPARTUM PANDEMIC

Sarah Burghauser

Kol Isha Publishing

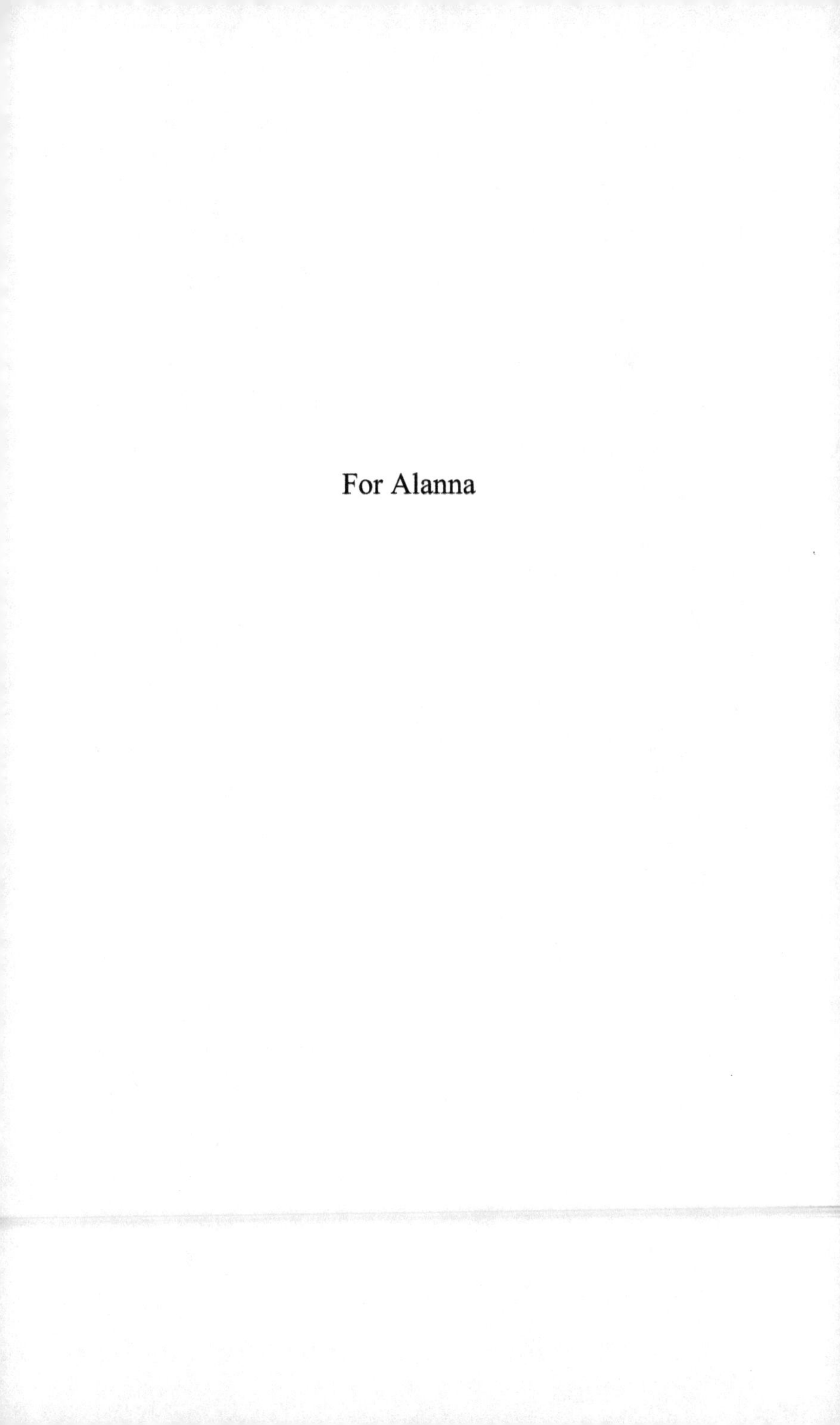

For Alanna

POSTPARTUM
PANDEMIC

Sarah Burghauser

This is what happens before the linea negra fades.

Vocabulary:

PPD
PPE
6-feet
Skin-to-skin

Quarantine
Quarantini
Quaranteam
Social distance
Shelter in place
Latch

Oxytocin
Pod
Pod up
Mask up
Lockdown
Mask

Curbside

Chord blood

Isolate

Why does nighttime smell different?

Like rain changing the barometric pressure, and water with its particular bacteria. The aroma of growing cells. Smells like my placenta pills I keep in the freezer.

The perfectly round milk stains on the sheets map where my body has been and how it's been moving in the night. The circumference of the stain marks minutes of sleep for me and for the baby. Like tree rings. Like bleeding out.

The Peri-bottle, the witch hazel, the pads. No time for ice packs this time around, though I'm longing to cool down. Everything is enflamed. Clothes are intolerable. Everything sticks and itches. Everything digs in and hangs wrong. Everything makes no sense on my body.
And what is my body now? It was always grotesque yet now it is monstrous. It was always unpredictable yet now it is chaotic. It was always a map yet now it is topographical. It was always needy yet now it is an emergency.

My eyes try to separate my vision. To get up with the
sidecar crib blocking my way, I roll to my side and inch to
the foot of the bed like I did when I was pregnant. And I
turn on the lights and open the bathroom window for fresh
air and I reach for my contact lenses. Now the day is
already over. Because it has begun.

I know he can feel all the sadness of the world through me.
Pouring out through my milk and my eyes and my vagina.
Milk is my second blood and blood is my vagina crying
and tears are just hose water filling up the kiddie pool.
Summertime.

Hormones are drugs with a different quality each time they
rev up inside the body. Depending on the source.
Hormones are experience. They journey you along until
you learn.

My labia split.
My hair is straight where the curls of my people once grew.
My breasts are gongs.
My fingertips turned into fly catchers.
My wrists are brittle branches.
There are ever creeping gaps between the shores of teeth
and rippling wavering gums and my migraines came back
and I am pubescent-scented with the acne to match what
we're doing here is utterly normal and that surprises me
every day.

I finally work up the courage to touch myself – just feel the
new contours. Gently. The whole thing raw. The whole
thing inflamed. I need a lube just to make contact without
wincing. I didn't know it was possible to have loose flaps
of skin growing from scar tissue. Or that labia could split
like this leaving me with three lips instead of two.

Whatever you do, don't look behind you. You may see
yourself living another life. Your life.

Wiping the groceries off every time feels
like keeping kosher or shomer Shabbos. We're never sure it
actually does anything. Yet we keep doing it. Like building
a fence around the Torah. Like using a cos sheini, or not
stirring the cholent on Shabbos. Like making sure no one
gets hurt in the home.

So this other woman. She is very young and blond. She is
waspy and unattached. She is straight and requires
indoctrination. My wife is giving her the grand tour. It
reminds me how I am so Semitic and kinky. I am so thick
and dark. I am so leaky. They bring my daughter on their
outings and I am at the house dripping milk into my
newborn's tiny mouth. I am so postpartum.

Dream. I hear someone say they are looking forward to
meeting my baby for the first time. That he is her son.

At 6 weeks he woke up to the world. But even before that, I could see in him that babies are born with all the emotions already inside them. Waiting to be poked. To be activated. And it doesn't take much to make that spark. He cycles through every expression just in his sleep, reacting to all the various sounds around him. All the sensations. A flicker of a smile preempts a furrowed brow and twitchy chin. It looks like he might cry, and then suddenly his face relaxes once more. Until the wind kicks up outside.

Fears:
That she ruined my life
That I ruined my life
That I am alone
That I am going to be alone for a long time
That I am never going to be able to support myself or my children
That having children was a mistake
That having the second child was a mistake
That I will never recognize myself again
That I am embarrassed about my choices
That I will never forgive myself
That I will never forgive her
That my children will hate me
That I will turn away from myself

That I will never dislodge the lump in my throat
That I know even less about life and myself than I ever
thought
That I will never have sex again
That I will never feel sexy again
That I am ruined
That my anger will rule me
That other people will only know her side of the story –
however she spins it
That I will never have the life I want
That my uncertainty is never ending
That I am ugly
That I am stupid
That I am weak

Postpartum pandemic.
Havoc.
Lost inside my body time.
The clock is suddenly spinning erratically.
I'm twice the person I used to be in body, yet half in spirit.
My toddler says, suspicious of my abdomen, "I came out of
Ima's belly. Baby brother came out of Ima's belly. So
many people came out of Ima's belly. Now there are no
people in Ima's belly." Am I really so empty? Am I really
so full?

Postpartum is anyway a pandemic on the body globe. Every inch of it vulnerable to the mistake of children and change.

This baby boy is the only thing that makes me happy these days. Him and his smile, his eyes twinkle. His knowing cries. I balance him in my neck like a violin and he wails on with such simplicity.
Holding onto his body. Holding on to my body by holding him close. I believe in you, boy. Like I believe in myself. As in, not at all, but the leap of faith is the only viable approach to such circumstances. To such histories. To such as it is.

It's not the kind of tired you get from just not getting enough sleep. It's an existential fatigue. On top of not getting enough sleep.

My auto correct cannot predict the word love. This is what happens when I try to write with a third the vocabulary I had when I left graduate school. My hair is beginning to fall out.

She offers her love only in a small dish so as to make the portion seem larger than it is.

The mind checks out, the partner checks out, words check out like an alibi.

I have survived my own body. I re-mind myself.
10

I need to leave the house. For 30 minutes. 20 minutes.

Is it Tai Chi? We are in a park. Green grass in the high
desert makes me anxious because I know how much water
it probably takes. Pandemic be dammed, there are elders
out here, masked and spread evenly apart. Their thin skin
covers their thick years. They bow slowly again and again
making languid movements with their arms, pushing the
wind away and then gathering it once more. They boundary
themselves expertly and gently find their little centers. I
can't help but wonder what their bellies look like. And their
breasts. What kind of work their bras are doing.
They together is she. And that's just the beginning for
them.
I try to keep the baby quiet. Against nature.

This baby is like the hummingbird, my backyard friend
who wants to share a meal. I can smell your oils. I can

smell your sugar. I can smell your yeast. Never noticing till now how thick such a tiny body can be. How energetic the extremities that make it fly. How devastating his smile can be as he beams up at me from the changing table, making eyes at me, smiling up up up at my pitiable efforts.

Trying to attribute this feeling of grief to what the pandemic stole. Not what she stole.

The configurations of nighttime. I rotate throughout the night and into the breaking of dawn. And I have come to be able to feel time measured and expressed by the arrangement of pillows and which side of my body I wake up on.

My heart pounds when I see the baby's erection. I try to point it down like they say, but even so, I can feel it through the diaper like a bad omen. I did not ask for this. I watch what I'm doing, making sure to cover him with a

cloth so he doesn't urinate on me and everything around us.
I know he can't help it. I fasten the diaper and finally look
at his face, which regards me with the most desperate and
apologetic of looks. And I know then, that it is not my job
to help him swim against the riptide of patriarchy, but
rather to help preserve his inherent sweetness.
No, I am not feeding him the sadness of the world. I am
just feeding him me.

Two kids. All night. Kicking me in the head, throwing their
legs and arms over me, or trying to suck on me. Sticking
their hands or feet down my pants, stealing my pillow,
twiddling my nipples making me want to bust out of my
own skin. I protect one kid from the other's body, with my
own body built like a wall down the bed, down the center
of my life, dividing me, straining my hips and back, my
neck a pile of bricks. It's not the newborn. It's the toddler
that touches me out. She head-butts me and twists my
earrings and plays with the skin on my neck and shoves her
knees into my back and plays with my hair. She is so sweet
when she cuddles me, I can't stand her. She laughs in her
sleep.

Seize the day. This is your time. One hour.

I risked it at the store. I went by myself, after the kids were
down, for the first time in months. I bought wipes and
soaps for hands, dishes, clothes, groceries, and the mail.
When I got home, everyone was crying for me.
So now I am nursing the baby in bed and arching my back
to calm the toddler too. I twist and shush and pull them
both close to me. I am hungry and I hope to be able to wash
my face before bed.
When I stepped back in, she stepped out to stargaze.

Pandemic: crisis, trauma, emergency.
My labia, my heart. My hair is falling out and I have more
than one belly.
This situation is worse than I thought. It goes to the very
core of what I thought was true. There is no working
through. It is like a pandemic because it infects every
corner of the body, of the life. But worse because there will
never be a vaccine. And so we're locked down. To our own
stories. To the mess she's made. To the dust gathering in

the corners, to the mold in the walls, to the infection she's
exhaled into our home.

I want to kill myself when:
— I think of all the ways I made myself vulnerable to her
— I think of my body
— I think about having sex again with anyone
— I think about what it means to honor and love ones own body like a parent
— I think about how far I've come and then starting over

Suddenly I feel the loneliness of Shabbat and Rosh Hashana. I see what life would be like divorced and I get the kids for Jewish holidays. And life is miserable.

Your body has been completely ravaged, your life has been turned upside down and inside out, and you are likely crawling out of your skin with worry and discomfort and love. You, whoever you are.

Pandemic: Global infection. Contamination of every part. In all the corners, like looking for chametz with a candle. If I can find it all, I'll burn it in the morning in a tin on the porch: my religiosity. My skin and flesh. The bones that moved during childbirth. Each strand of my hair that has fallen out. I want to burn.

A dream in which a former lover points out that my hair is now straight. I shrug because she'll gloat if I tell her it was childbirth that permanently flattened my curls. She rejected me when I got pregnant the first time because she knew I was already on my way to becoming different. And I have that feeling of disorientation. Of having to switch instantly from trusting someone with your life, to not trusting them at all. This change is illogical and probably has nothing to do with me. Except what if it does. Who am I really? They made me doubt myself. My whole self.

My vulva. That birthed my first. That stretched, but not enough. A vulva that had to break itself open without any drugs, without any oil or coaxing. Without any fanfare or foreplay. Without any of the trappings of wet sex, hot mouth feel, or gentle love. My vulva tore. My perineum tore. My vaginal walls tore. My labia tore. And none of the stitches took. This is the very bottom of my belly, the very core of me. It is mangled.

The relationship feels way the house does when you're getting ready to move out. To release it back to the landlord. The way dust begins to pile in all the creases and corners. The way the bathroom collects loose hair faster than usual. The way the stove never gets clean. The way we decide to get rid of the things we didn't realize until now that we don't need. Dishes don't matter. Bed making doesn't matter nor do the sheets. The mirrors are clouded. The way we begin to eat take out and frozen foods more because cooking is something you do in a home. Not a place you are getting ready to leave. The only thing I am excluded from is that which I feel most connected to.

We're sitting in the kitchen, living room, bedroom, bath, and the toddler keeps saying, "I want to go home." She doesn't know what she means. Except that she does. And so do I.

So now, I'm going to have to date. In this body. With this bitterness. I used to be a person who was a different person. Now I want to smash my body like glass.

My breasts are massive. My breasts are mighty. My breasts are bashful elephants fluttering their ears. There is no fullness, really. Just the maniacal weakness of skin barely holding my flesh in. It's all trying to escape. It's all out there and won't be contained. I hunch over again like I did when I was younger and I was only beginning to understand my body. I am pubescent again. And postpartum at once.

The linea negra never fully fades.
I want to kill her in her sleep. I want to throw myself out a window. I'm nursed until the sun comes up and then I'm nursed some more. I'm taking care of business. That line runs down the middle of everything. My belly has a border. A wall that won't let go. Sutures of color. On one side there was me. And on the other side, me. That line could be

magical. Or it could be a brand.

Executive function makes me nervous. My mind does backflips to understand what is happening and how to keep myself, at any given moment, from kicking in a wall. Because I'm sleeping in the bed that she made for herself. And I don't recognize the scent on the pillowcase.

What does pandemic mean in the postpartum time? What does a new life mean in a landscape of sickness? What does fear mean when there is nothing to salvage? What does blood mean when I am so thirsty? Branded, tagged for motherhood. My wings clipped.

Divorce, lies, pandemic.

Children, chains, pandemic.
Mask, finances, pandemic.
Split, ravage, pandemic.
Wine, smash, pandemic.
Body, attack, pandemic.
Clammy, calamity, pandemic.
Alone, release, pandemic.
Tear, tear, pandemic.
Lochia, lockdown, pandemic
Home, fire, pandemic.
Night and day, pandemic.
Change, force, pandemic.
Gird, glass, pandemic.
Cruel, mire, pandemic.
Love, letdown, pandemic.
Over and over pandemic.

So much so that I saved that bottle for last.
So much so that the bottle wouldn't break.
So much so that it bounced back at me off the rubbled
cinderblock.
So much so that I stumbled on my way up the hill to
retrieve it.
So much so that I tripped and fell.
So much so that I tore the maternity pants I was still
wearing and cut my knee underneath.
So much so that I only noticed because of the blood on my
hands.
So much.
So much so that I finally broke it and it shattered
unsatisfyingly.
So much so that I squatted to gather everything left in me.
So much so that I screamed, "fuck" until my vision went
blurry.
So much so that my mask got stuck in my mouth like a
bit.
So much so that my hands came up in front of me like
dancing, and then to my face.
So much so that I collapsed in front of the mess in the line
of fire, on scattered shards of glass, with my mask in my
mouth, disoriented from anger, clouded by grief, bleeding
and sobbing, keeping an eye on the time to get back and
breastfeed my baby.
So much so that I finished my whiskey shot before getting
back in the car.

22

So much.
So much for marriage.
So much for family.
So much for honesty.
So much for tenderness.
So much for affection and health.
So much for intimacy and laughter.
So much for grounded-ness and love.
So much for loyalty.
So much for energy and strength in my body.
So much for breaking the cycle of unhappy homes.
So much for trust.

Think not about the relentlessness of the contractions, but rather about their mercy. They have both qualities. The enormity of them. The fullness and depth of them like ocean water in a storm. But think about the briefness of their most intense moments. The forgiveness of the lulls. Think about the grace. Think about the wisdom of the body. Be your body. Re-mind yourself.

I tear the snaps on my nursing top open like a superhero. "I got you," I say.

Snacks by the fistful, which is not as big as it sounds. The fist is small and whatever goes in gets crushed. Laundry by the bucket-load in that godforsaken apartment washer that I fill from the tub then rinse by hand and hang to dry. I wash masks separately, wash work clothes separately. Everyone's in the bathroom at the same time for a bath for the toilet for the laundry for hand washing. The baby bouncer, the step stool, the legs and feet, the sitting on top of the toilet lid. And there's the diaper changes, the books we read, the walks to our mailbox and throwing pebbles in the backyard. That's quarantine. What we do all day. The naps on my chest in the carrier, the drool and spit up between my breasts, over my shoulders and down my back. My cracked hands and feet and lips. The hats and shoes and bending down while wearing the sleeping infant. Please don't wake him up, please please please. The lunchbox and water bottles, assembling the double stroller and stuffing the diaper bag underneath and pushing all that poundage up the subtle inclines of the neighborhood.

Before I had kids I was vital. I could have had her. I could have had her. I could have had her or even him. Now I can't even have a glass of wine in peace.

I want to remind her every day that I hate her. How much she is fucking up. Every day I want to slice her open a little. So there's no opportunity for a scab to form. Like on my skin. Like my body can take. Like my blood can make.

I know that my body can turn blood into milk, so there has to be a way forward while I figure out how to let go of my anger. The time it takes, what I will have to spend, calculating my reserves, my mind repeats: I did not ask for this.

I have survived my father. I have survived my friends and three rapists. I have survived the cliff in a truck when I was too tired to drive. I have survived my own desire to make it all stop. I have survived the insistence that I put others' needs before my own. I have survived the fear of my own voice. I have survived being rejected by close friends. I have survived mine and others' dishonesty. I have survived childbirth. Twice. I have survived being alone and vulnerable. I have survived not knowing where I was going to sleep. I have survived the most difficult of conversations. I have survived being triggered and re-traumatized. I have survived. Whips and unpredictability. I have survived my own mind.

Our conversations are punctuated by baby wake ups. We're never finished. A snack left cold on the counter because I'm not hungry anymore. The infant, the toddler. They all want to know where I am. They all want my body. They all want a piece of me. My arms, my neck, my breasts, and what is inside my body, too. What a generation will remember.

The winter sun never quite rises till midday.

And even then, its heat is uneven. The baby is flapping his arms and rolling this way and that, though his eyes are still closed. He whimpers and groans, but he's not upset. His body is just speaking to him, and he's trying to speak back. His subconscious is developing right before my eyes. I stroke his cheek and kiss all over his face. He yawns and I put my nose right into is mouth and inhale deeply. I whisper, "hi baby," and he opens his eyes and smiles. Those first two teeth have changed the shape of his smirk. I know that once more teeth come in, the shape of his whole face will change and I'll begin to see flashes of my uncles and brothers in his appearance. Flashes of me if I were a boy. I unzip his sleep sack and lift him sideways onto my abdomen so he's resting on my breast. He shifts his head and latches. Sometimes when we're in bed, he throws himself at me and lands with his face on my stomach. He coos and blows raspberries on me and I can feel my skin vibrating under him. But now he's feeding, staring at me with the one eye that can see over my breast.

Now it is quiet and still, but I know the day has begun. The expanse of the next 13 hours hits me. I start thinking about breakfast and naptime and then lunch and activities between snacks, another naptime, and how my body is going to withstand wearing the baby in the carrier for hours. How I am going to nurse and entertain him, help him practice crawling and pulling himself up, how I'm going to also run the toddler ragged today so that she's tired enough tonight – so that she'll have learned something today. One thing at least. Even if it's just that I love her. That I am not going anywhere. Just me and the kids. I think about whether or not I'll be able to withstand them both fussing and crying long enough – five minutes? – for me to take a shower. There is still no place to take them. No library, no baby-gym, no playground, no cafes, no play dates. Just me and the kids.

The toddler stirs. Here we go. I wonder how much time I can reasonably let her watch videos today so that I can nap the baby, study, work, do laundry, make phone calls, eat. I look over at her and our eyes immediately meet and she smiles her gorgeous melty smile and her eyes are crusted and her hair is wickedly tangled and she has that dreamy look in her eyes and the first words out of her mouth this morning are, "I love you Ima." She throws her leg over me and it lands on the baby's head. He unlatches and looks up at his big sister. I readjust my body and then the babies' bodies so that I'm holding them both. She wants to give her baby brother a kiss so I pull him over to the other side of my body so the siblings are next to each other. She puts him in a loving headlock. "He loves me," she says. "Yes darling, he loves you so much." The baby is always so amused by her, even first thing in the morning, and he gives her an even bigger smile than he gave me. The enormity of this time hits me, as it often does, catching me off guard. A pandemic still yet unresolved. So many moments I just don't know how to interpret. Are they peaceful? Are they lonely? Are they scary? Are they empowering?

Now I'm changing diapers and flipping pancakes and trying to listen to the news above toddler complaints and demands, and the baby singing from the floor as he tries to coordinate his limbs to grab a toy just out of reach. Though my breasts still run the show, my milk is no longer leaking. I have just enough and not too much. I have learned what size jeans I now wear, though I'm not yet used to the way my bellies look and feel under denim. Or any other fabric for that matter. I have taken up exfoliating when I have the time. With kids quarantined, dawn is the harbinger of bedtime because the day is programed. The schedule is sacred. Our stability depends on it.

My tummy is lumpy, the linea negra still swimming up and down, though now, a little father beneath the surface of skin. I have learned how to withstand the night when I am trying to work and settle the babies and read and write and settle the babies when they wake, make phone calls and clean, settle the babies in the bedroom again, and do dishes until midnight and then breastfeed until dawn. I have learned how to create more hours in the day. It's not that I've found rhythm. I've just found words. I've just found me in the rubble. And I'm not yet in focus. But I'll see what the rest of the day holds.

About the Author

Sarah Burghauser is a New Mexico-based writer and teacher. She holds an MFA from Calarts, where she has also taught. Sarah has been awarded fellowships with the MacDowell Colony, Lambda Literary Foundation, and Vermont Studio Center. Her first book, *Infringe*, is a lyric coming-of-age tale about being a queer Jew, and the places where sex and spiritual well being meet.

www.ingramcontent.com/pod-product-compliance
Lightning Source LLC
Chambersburg PA
CBHW031249130726
47988CB00008B/3308